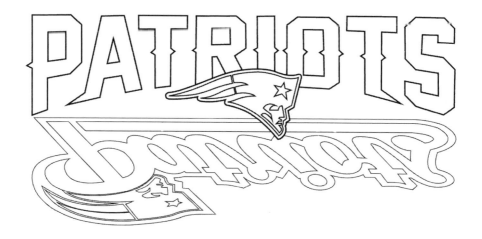

FEBRUARY 5 2017

Location:

NRG Stadium Houston, Texas

LI 51st Super Bowl

Broadcasting Network:

FOX

Atlanta Falcons

Cost of 30-second commercial:

$5.02 Million

players

legends

LOGOS

DESIGN CENTER

PATRIOTS
PLAYERS

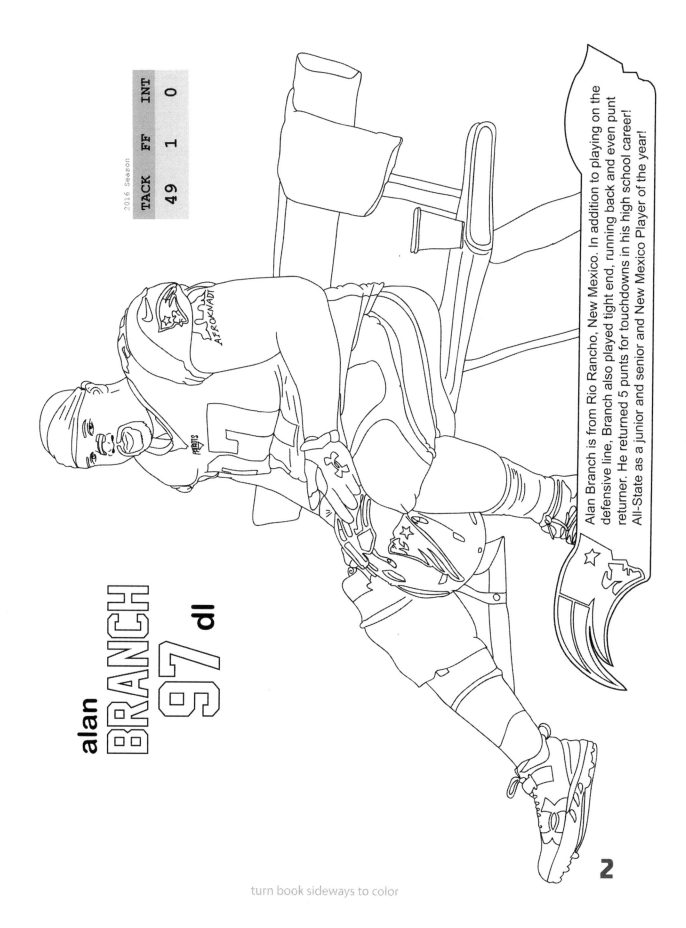

alan
BRANCH
97 dl

2016 Season

TACK	FF	INT
49	1	0

Alan Branch is from Rio Rancho, New Mexico. In addition to playing on the defensive line, Branch also played tight end, running back and even punt returner. He returned 5 punts for touchdowns in his high school career! All-State as a junior and senior and New Mexico Player of the year!

2

chris
HOGAN
15 wr

2016 Season

REC	YDS	TD
38	680	4

Chris Hogan grew up in Wyckoff, New Jersey and played football and lacrosse in high school. He was 1st team all-state in both sports, and attended Penn State to play lacrosse (and graduated). With a year left of athletic eligibility, Chris enrolled at Monmouth University to play one year of college football.

chris
LONG
95 de

2016 Season

TACK	FF	SACK
35	1	4

Chris Long was born in Santa Monica, California. As a senior in high school, Chris recorded 91 tackles, 23 for a loss, 15 sacks and played in the HS All-American Bowl! He went to the University of Virginia, becoming an All-American and the 2nd pick in the 2008 NFL draft! Chris is the son of NFL great Howie Long!

4

danny
AMENDOLA
80 wr

2016 Season

REC	YDS	TD
23	243	4

Danny Amendola grew up in Houston, Texas and went to Texas Tech University where he played with fellow NFL receiver Michael Crabtree! His senior season Danny had 109 catches, 1,245 yards and 6 TD's.

5

devin
MCCOURTY
32 fs/cb

2016 Season

TACK	FF	SACK
83	1	1

Devin McCourty was born in New York and attended school in New Jersey. He was also a point guard on his high school basketball team. Devin received a football scholarship to Rutgers University, as did his twin brother - fellow NFL'er Jason McCourty who currently plays cornerback for the Titans!

dont'a
HIGHTOWER
54 lb

2016 Season

TACK	FF	INT
65	1	0

Dont'a Hightower was born and went to high school in Lewisburg, Tennessee. He first was noticed as a football star his sophomore year in high school when the team's starting running back quit. With four games left in the season, Dont'a rushed for over 1,000 yards! 1st team All-American in college at Alabama.

TACK	FF	SACK
33	0	5

jabaal
SHEARD
93 dl

Jabaal Sheard is from Hollywood, Florida where he was a standout football and track and field athlete. Jabaal was clocked at 4.6 seconds in the 40-yard dash at a Nike combine prior to his senior season (which is incredible for his size). He played college football for the University of Pittsburgh.

8

james
WHITE
28rb

2016 Season

ATT	YDS	TD
39	166	0

James White was born and raised in Fort Lauderdale, Florida. He was part of the 2008 St. Thomas Aquinas high school "National Championship" team. James rushed for over 1,000 yards and 20 TD's his senior year despite splitting time with fellow NFL running back, Giovani Bernard!

TRADED

jamie
COLLINS
91 lb

2016 Season

TACK	FF	INT
112	2	2

Jamie Collins was traded to the Browns in October, 2016. Before then, he was an athletic and talented linebacker for the Patriots. Jamie was born and raised in Mississippi and played quarterback, receiver and safety before becoming a linebacker in high school! He played college football for Southern Miss.

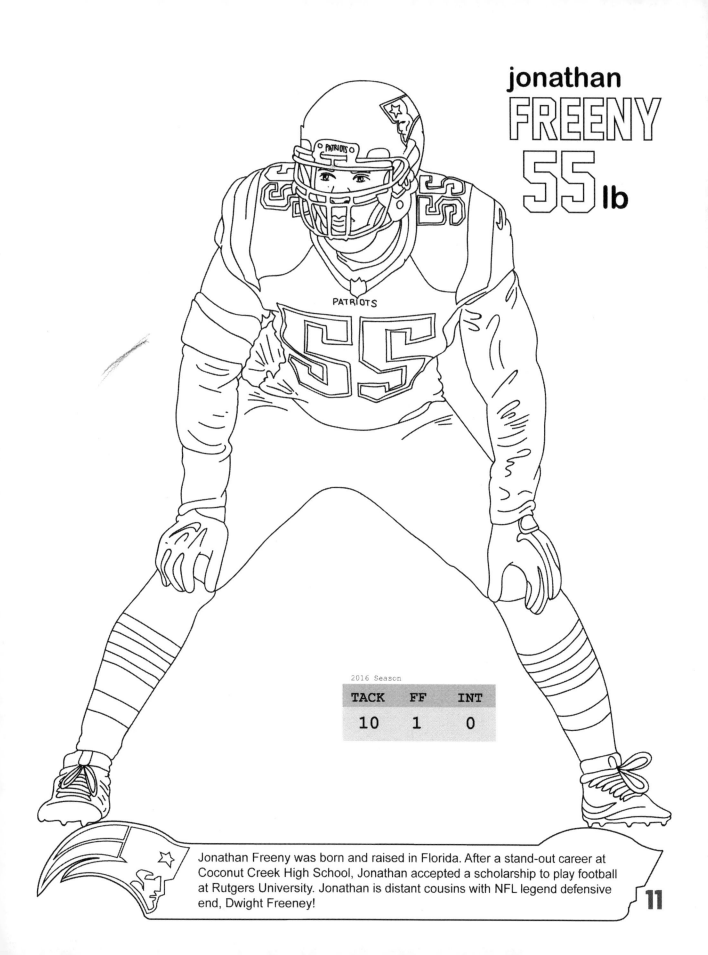

jonathan
FREENY
55 lb

2016 Season

TACK	FF	INT
10	1	0

Jonathan Freeny was born and raised in Florida. After a stand-out career at Coconut Creek High School, Jonathan accepted a scholarship to play football at Rutgers University. Jonathan is distant cousins with NFL legend defensive end, Dwight Freeny!

11

julian
EDELMAN
11 wr

2016 Season

2016 Season		
REC	YDS	TD
98	1106	3

Julian Edelman is from California and was a quarterback in high school and college! At Kent State University, Julian was a three-year starter at QB. His senior year he led the team in passing (1,820 yards) and rushing (1,370 yards)! He converted to wide receiver his rookie year with the Patriots.

legarrette
BLOUNT
29 rb

2016 Season

ATT	YDS	TD
299	1161	18

LeGarrette Blount was born and raised in Florida. In high school, he was a four year starter and 2nd-team All-State as a senior, however he was hardly recruited so LeGarrette attended a junior college to continue playing football. He once again became a star and received a scholarship from the University of Oregon.

13

logan
RYAN
26 cb

2016 Season

TACK	FF	SACK
92	1	2

Logan Ryan is from New Jersey. He was a star athlete in high school, earning all-state honors at both quarterback and defensive back! Logan later became an All-American at Rutgers University and decided to turn pro after his junior season. He was drafted in the 3rd round (83rd overall) in the 2013 Draft.

malcolm
BUTLER
21 cb

2016 Season

TACK	FF	INT
63	1	4

Malcolm Butler was born and raised in Vicksburg, Mississippi. Despite not playing football his sophomore and junior years, Malcolm earned a scholarship to play at Hinds Community College and later enrolled at the University of West Alabama. In 2014, Malcolm signed with the Patriots after going undrafted.

malcolm
MITCHELL
19 wr

2016 Season

REC	YDS	TD
32	401	4

Malcolm Mitchell was born and raised in Valdosta, Georgia. Malcolm played at the University of Georgia from 2011 to 2015. Upon graduating, he finished third in school history with 174 receptions for 2,350 yards and 16 touchdowns! He was selected in the fourth round of the 2016 NFL Draft.

malcom
BROWN
90 dl

2016 Season

TACK	FF	INT
50	1	0

Malcom Brown was born and raised in Brenham, Texas. He was a three-sport athlete in high school, playing football, basketball and track. Malcom was considered a five-star recruit and was ranked as the second best defensive tackle in his class. He was an All-American at the University of Texas.

martellus
BENNETT
88 te

2016 Season

REC	YDS	TD
55	701	7

Martellus Bennett was born in California, but grew up in Texas where he starred in both football and basketball. As a high school senior, he was all-state in football and averaged 23 points and 8 rebounds a game in basketball! Martellus even declared for the 2005 NBA draft but chose college instead!

18

patrick
CHUNG
23 ss

2016 Season		
TACK	FF	INT
91	0	1

Patrick Chung was born in Jamaica and later attended school in California. He has four brothers and three sisters. He played college football for the University of Oregon and was a Freshman All-American. Patrick holds the defensive record for starting more games straight (51) than any other player in Oregon history.

19

rob
GRONKOWSKI
87 te

2016 Season

REC	YDS	TD
25	540	3

Rob "GRONK" Gronkowski was raised in Williamsville, New York. He played football and basketball in high school and was one of the top tight end recruits in the nation. He later played for the University of Arizona where he received All-American honors. Gronk was the 42nd pick in the 2010 NFL Draft.

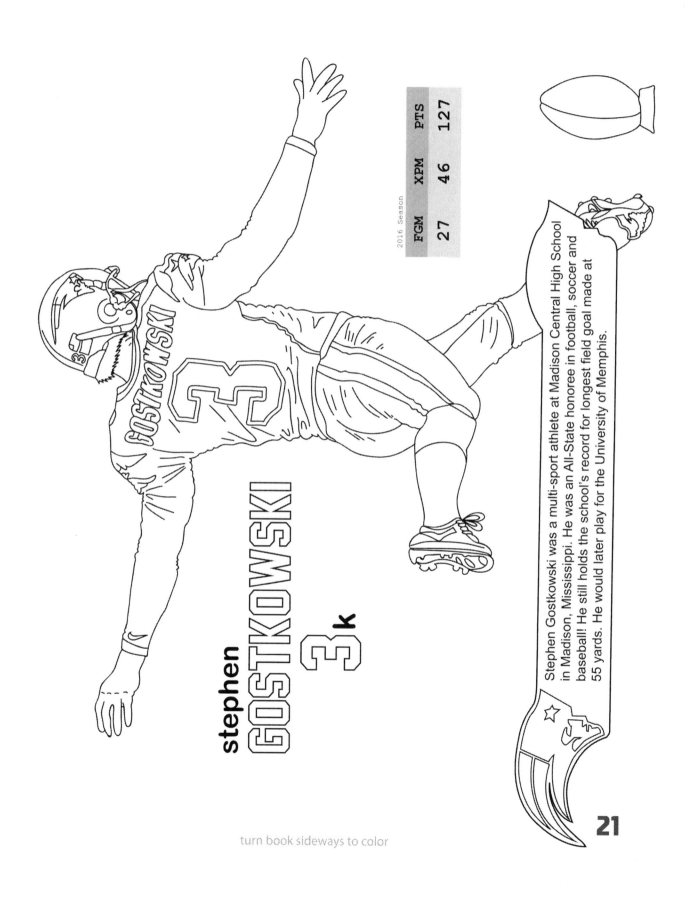

stephen
GOSTKOWSKI
3k

2016 Season		
FGM	**XPM**	**PTS**
27	46	127

Stephen Gostkowski was a multi-sport athlete at Madison Central High School in Madison, Mississippi. He was an All-State honoree in football, soccer and baseball! He still holds the school's record for longest field goal made at 55 yards. He would later play for the University of Memphis.

turn book sideways to color

tom
BRADY
12 qb

2016 Season		
CMP	YDS	CMP%
291	3554	67.4
TD	INT	RAT
28	2	112.2

Tom Brady was born and raised in San Mateo, California and has three older sisters. Tom was known for being a great baseball player, playing catcher in high school. He was even drafted by the Montreal Expos in 1995 before deciding to pursue his passion - football- and attening the University of Michigan.

22

bill
BELICHICK
head coach

2016 Season

WIN	LOSS
14	2

Career

WIN	LOSS
261	125

Bill Belichick was born in Nashville, Tennessee and raised in Maryland. His father was a football coach too! Bill played center and tight end at Wesleyan University. After graduating college he was paid $25 a week (in 1975) as an asistant to the head coach of the Colts. 6x Super Bowl Winner, 3x NFL coach of the year!

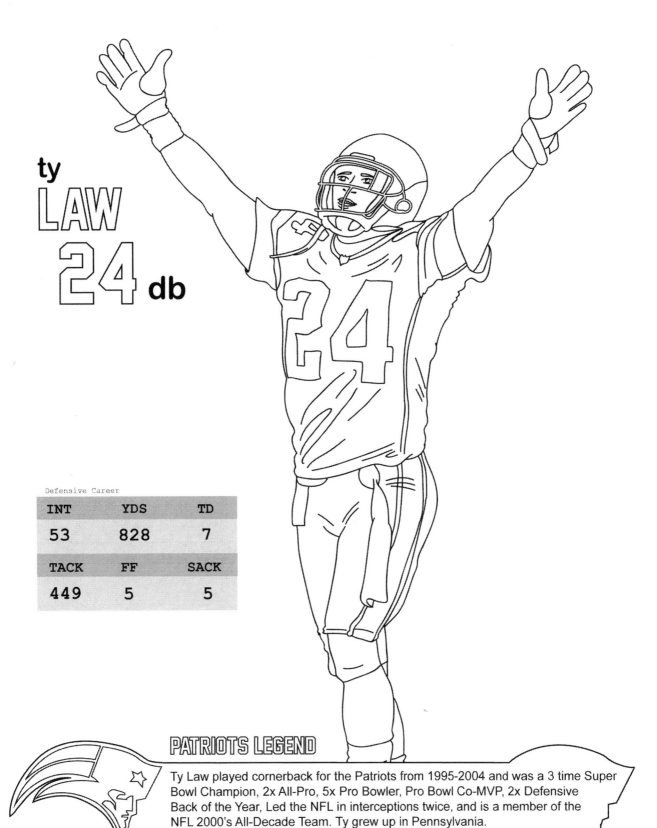

ty
LAW
24 db

Defensive Career

INT	YDS	TD
53	828	7
TACK	FF	SACK
449	5	5

PATRIOTS LEGEND

Ty Law played cornerback for the Patriots from 1995-2004 and was a 3 time Super Bowl Champion, 2x All-Pro, 5x Pro Bowler, Pro Bowl Co-MVP, 2x Defensive Back of the Year, Led the NFL in interceptions twice, and is a member of the NFL 2000's All-Decade Team. Ty grew up in Pennsylvania.

24

drew
BLEDSOE
11 qb

Career Stats		
CMP	YDS	CMP%
3839	44611	57.2
TD	INT	RAT
251	206	77.1

PATRIOTS LEGEND

Drew Bledsoe played for the Patriots from 1993-2001 (selected 1st Pick in '93). He was a Super Bowl Champion, 4x Pro Bowler, 2x AFC Champion and led the NFL in passing yards (in 1994). In 2011, Drew was voted by Patriots fans into the Patriots Hall of Fame. Drew grew up in Washington State.

randy
MOSS
81 wr

Career Stats

REC	YDS
982	15292

AVG	TDS
15.6	156

PATRIOTS LEGEND

Randy Moss played for the Patriots from 2007-2010. In 2007- his first year with the Patriots - he recorded 98 catches for 1,493 yards and an NFL record 23 receiving touchdowns! 6x Pro Bowler, 4x First-team All-Pro, NFL Rookie of the year, 5x NFL receiving TD leader, and considered one of best WR's in history.

26

troy
BROWN
80 wr

Career Stats			
REC	YDS	AVG	TDS
557	6366	11.4	31

PATRIOTS LEGEND

Troy Brown played his entire NFL career with the Patriots (1993-2007) and was a 3x Super Bowl Champion. Although Troy only made one Pro Bowl, he was a wide receiver and return man who was feared around the league for over a decade. He is a member of the College Football Hall of Fame (Marshall).

LOGOS

28

GIANTS

29

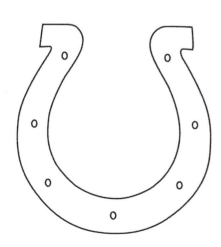

30

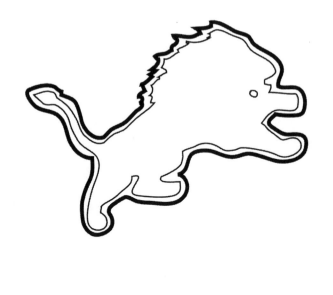

31

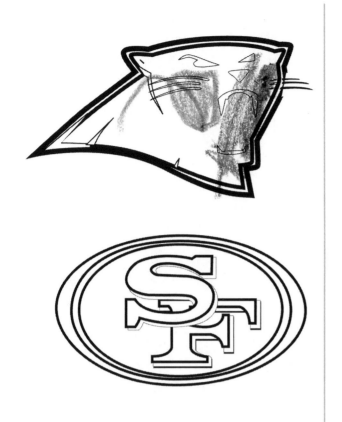

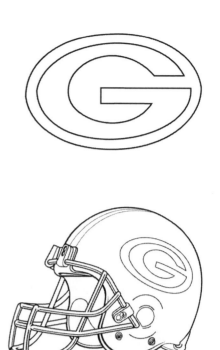

32

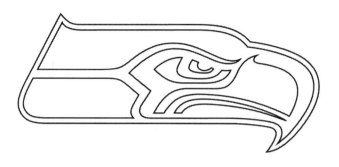

SEAHAWKS
SEATTLE

33

12 TOM BRADY

DESIGN CENTER

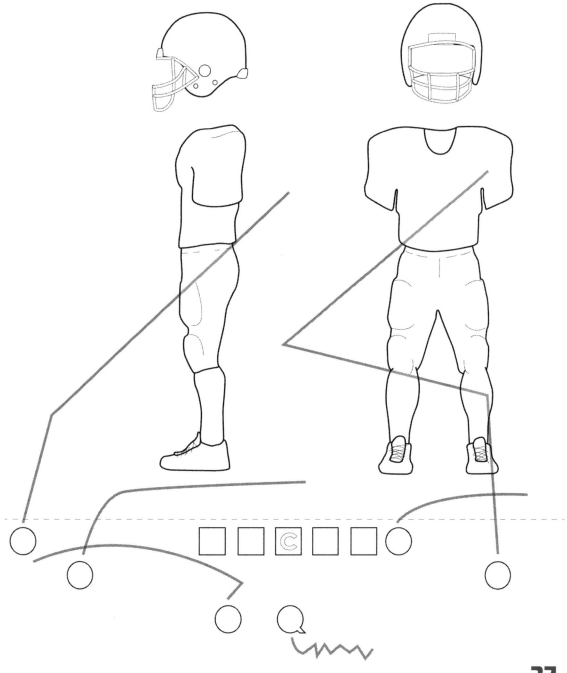

38

39

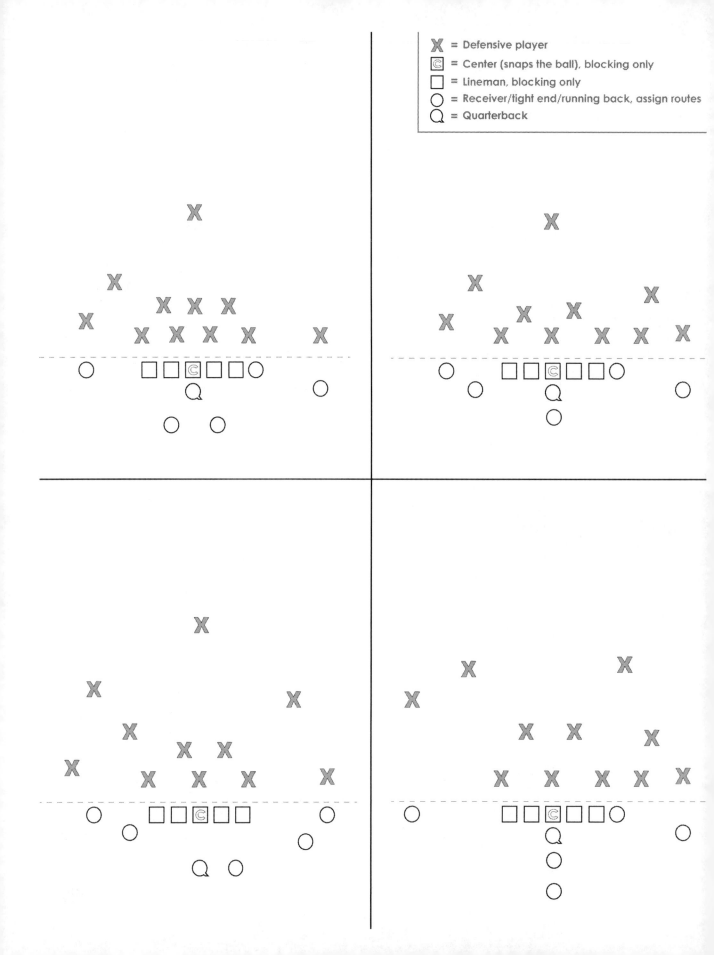

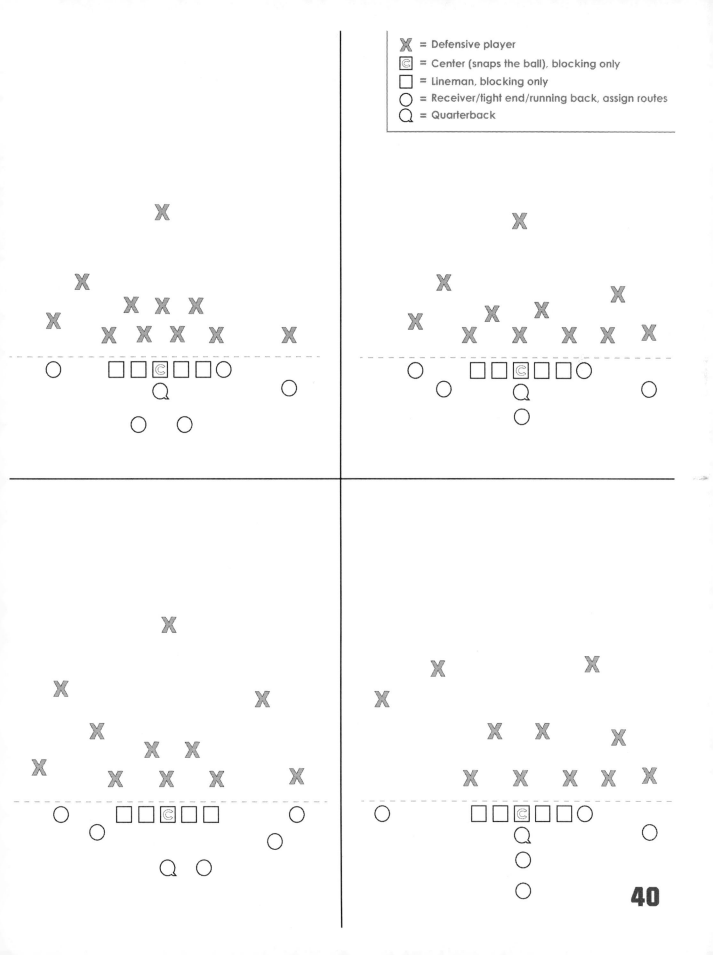

DRAW YOUR OWN
(You get 11 *total* players)

	Legend
ⓒ	= Center (snaps the ball), blocking only
□	= Lineman, blocking only
○	= Receiver/tight end/running back, assign routes
Q	= Quarterback

□ □ ⓒ □ □
Q

□ □ ⓒ □ □
Q

□ □ ⓒ □ □
Q

□ □ ⓒ □ □

Q

□ □ ⓒ □ □

Q

□ □ ⓒ □ □
Q

DRAW YOUR OWN
(You get 11 *total* players)

- ☐ = Center (snaps the ball), blocking only
- ☐ = Lineman, blocking only
- ○ = Receiver/tight end/running back, assign routes
- Q = Quarterback

41

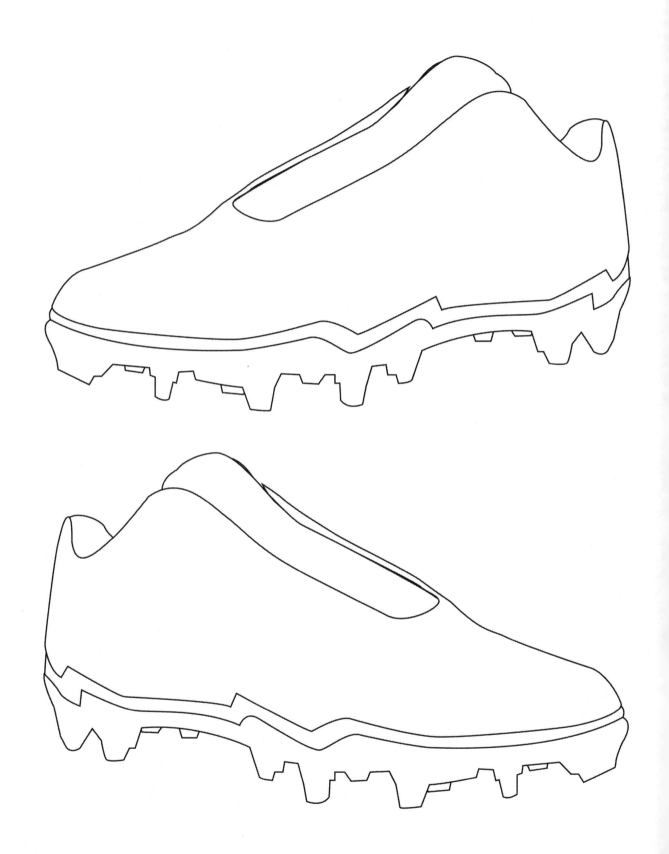

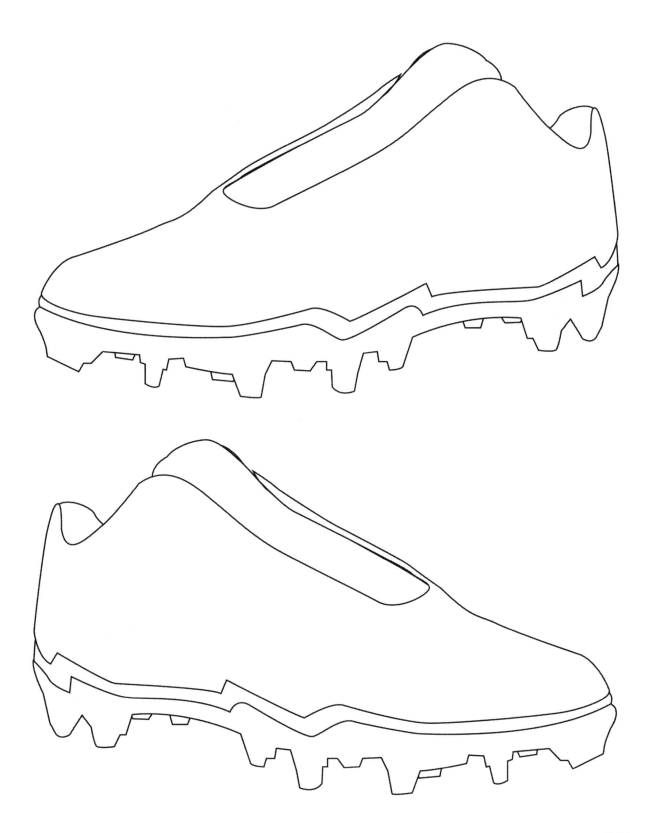

43

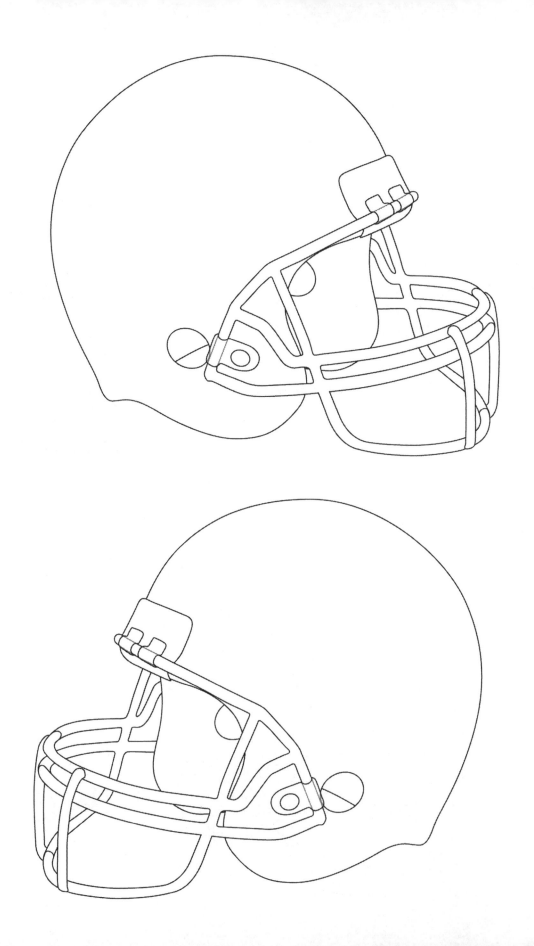

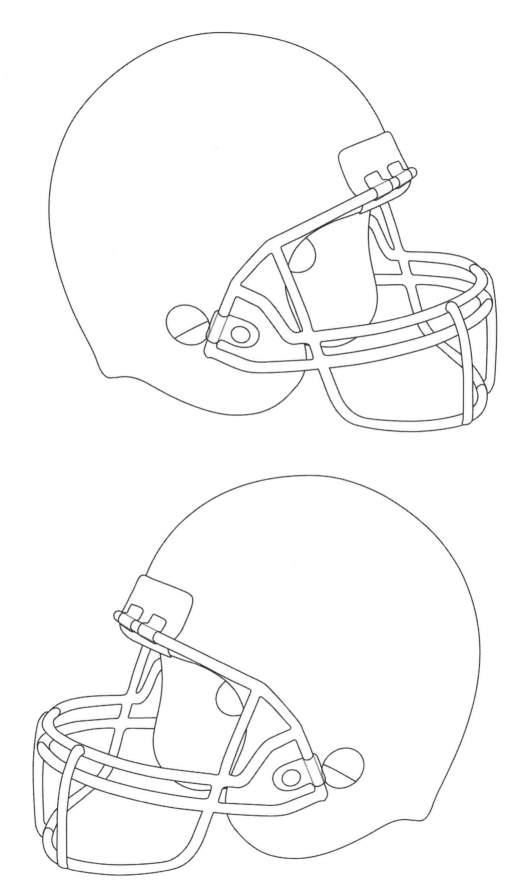

44

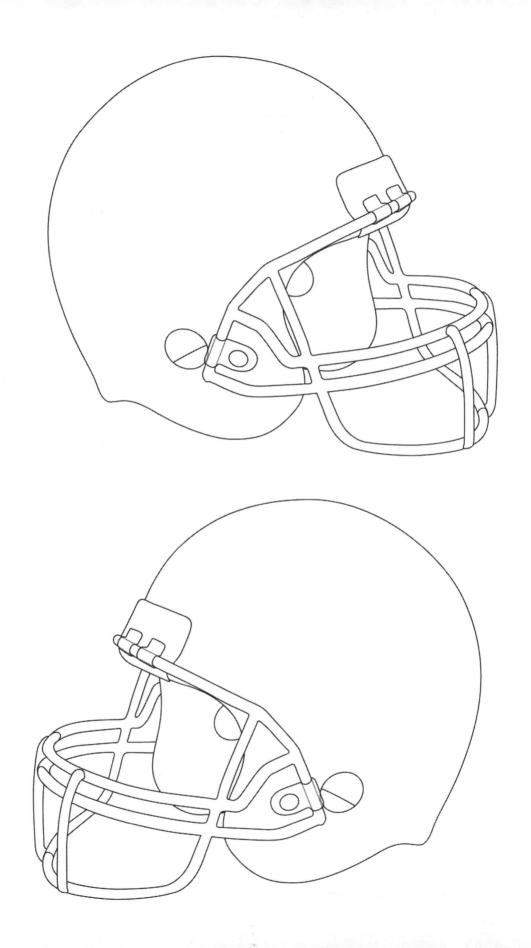

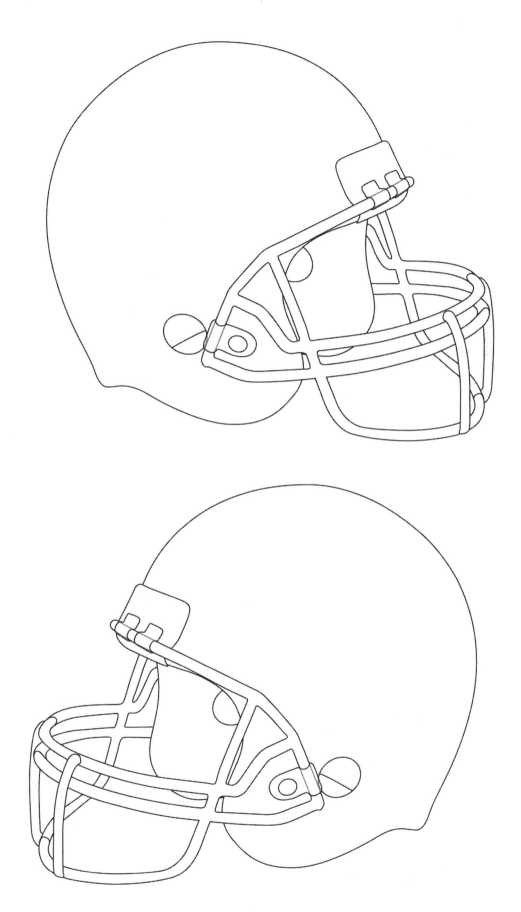

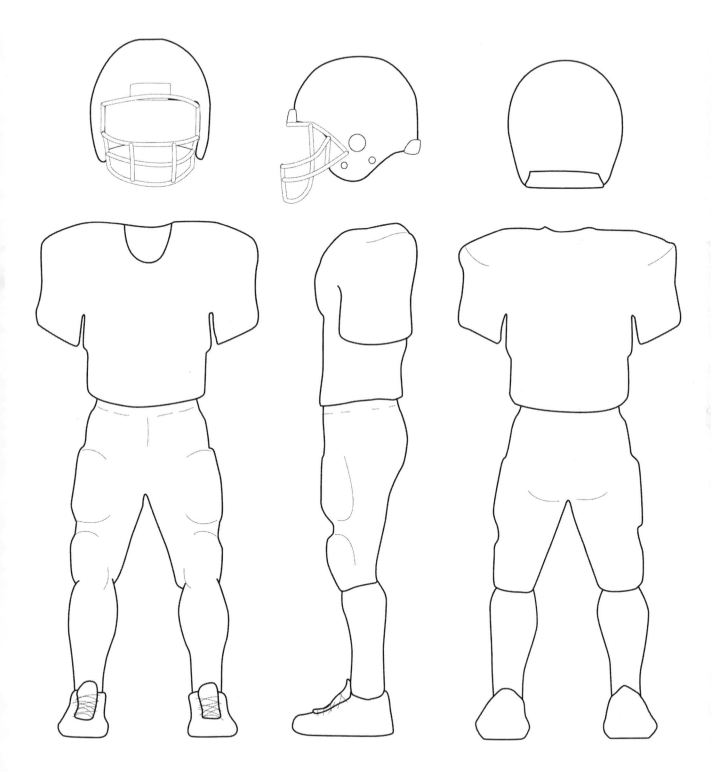

46

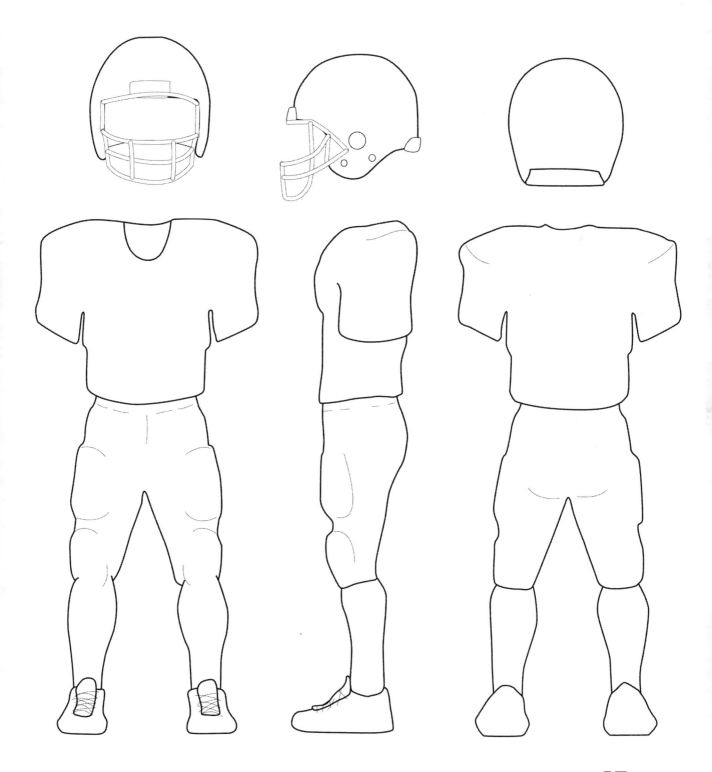

Made in the USA
Lexington, KY
23 February 2017